IMAGES
of America

MORGANTON AND BURKE COUNTY

Table Rock Mountain, Burke County's most noteworthy natural landmark, has loomed over Morganton and the entire Foothills region of North Carolina for centuries. It is believed that Table Rock inspired author Jules Verne to create the terrifying mountain known as the "Great Eyrie" in his 1904 book, *Master of the World*. A large part of Verne's novel is set near Morganton in the Blue Ridge Mountains that preside over the northern part of the county.

IMAGES
of America

MORGANTON AND BURKE COUNTY

H. Eugene Willard

Copyright © 2001 by H. Eugene Willard.
ISBN 978-1-5316-0936-8

Published by Arcadia Publishing
Charleston, South Carolina

Library of Congress Catalog Card Number: 2001091444

For all general information contact Arcadia Publishing at:
Telephone 843-853-2070
Fax 843-853-0044
E-Mail sales@arcadiapublishing.com
For customer service and orders:
Toll-Free 1-888-313-2665

Visit us on the Internet at www.arcadiapublishing.com

Morgantonians love a parade, which has long been a good excuse to get dressed up and meet friends and neighbors downtown, such as in this Fourth of July celebration in 1919.

Contents

Introduction		7
1.	Courthouse Square	9
2.	Downtown Morganton	17
3.	Churches and Schools	37
4.	Burke County at Work	53
5.	Burke County at Play	77
6.	The Waldenses Settlement	91
7.	Landmarks: Then and Now	105
8.	Burke County Distinctions	119
Acknowledgments		128

INTRODUCTION

Created out of Rowan County on June 1, 1777, Burke County originally extended west to the Continental Divide. After a final treaty with the Cherokees following the Indian Wars of 1776–1777, the county extended to the Tennessee border. Between 1790 and 1911, a number of other counties were carved from "Big Burke," but the county remains the largest, geographically, in the western half of the state, with slightly more than 500 square miles of land.

The Catawba River bisects the county, and the 12-mile Linville Gorge Wilderness Area claims the northwesternmost part of the county. A series of spurs of the Blue Ridge of the Appalachian Mountains dominates the skyline, and they are appropriately named by their unusual rock formations: Sitting Bear, Hawksbill, Table Rock, and the Chimneys.

Settled by hearty Scotch-Irish, English, and German pioneers, the county became the hub of the region, and the county seat was established at the town of Alder Springs, later named Morgan or Morgansborough (after Revolutionary War hero General Daniel Morgan). It was finally shortened to Morganton.

Traders and trappers had long traversed the area, but Morganton prospered as a stagecoach crossroads and, later, as a prominent railroad stop. Yeoman farming gave way to tanning and lumbering (which took advantage of the availability of animal hides and huge stands of native timber) as the chief local industries. These evolved into shoe and furniture manufacturing, and the county remains home to Drexel Heritage and Henredon Furniture Industries.

In 1893, a large contingent of immigrant Waldenses (Protestant Italians from the high valleys of the Cottian Alps) settled in the county in Valdese, the second largest municipality in Burke County.

The Burke County Courthouse, erected in the mid-1830s, became the center of government, and in the mid-19th century, the North Carolina State Supreme Court held its summer sessions in Morganton so members could escape the heat of the capital city for the cooler climate in the Foothills. The court sessions drew a number of lawyers, lobbyists, and their entourages, creating in Morganton an elevated cultural season of public and private entertaining.

Later in the century, to alleviate the overcrowding of the state asylum for the mentally ill in Raleigh, the North Carolina General Assembly created the Western Insane Asylum of North Carolina—later to be known as Broughton Hospital—in Morganton in 1883. The following year, the General Assembly established the North Carolina School for the Deaf in Morganton. The school, still the largest of its kind in the United States, housed some 500 students at its peak enrollment in the 1960s. These two institutions, along with a number of other state facilities, have given Morganton the distinction of being called the "Western Capital." In fact there are more state employees in Burke County than anywhere else in North Carolina, except for the capital city, Raleigh, and Chapel Hill, the site of the University of North Carolina.

This book is a pictorial retrospective of the past century. It is by no means a complete collection, but we expect the photographs selected may rekindle images of eras long past. We also hope that some of the people and places included in this volume will remind us all of the rich legacy left to those of us who have chosen to make Burke County our home.

One
COURTHOUSE SQUARE

The first courthouse for Burke County, constructed during the mid-1830s, is the oldest public building in North Carolina west of Salisbury. It has undergone several major changes and upgrades over the years. Its original stone facade was covered with a stucco exterior in 1885, and in 1903, an extensive remodeling included the addition of an ornamental cupola. A stone wall was erected around the Courthouse Square in 1933. When a new courthouse was completed on Green Street in 1976, the functioning court was moved there, a block away; the old building was renovated in the early 1980s and is home today to Historic Burke Foundation. This view, taken from Union Street, also shows oblique parking that was eliminated in 1979 when the street became one-way for westbound traffic.

Until the advent of the automobile, Court Week was a time for camping out near the Burke County Courthouse in Morganton. The North Carolina Supreme Court held its summer sessions here from 1847 to 1861 so judges, lawyers, and their entourages could escape the seasonal heat in Raleigh for the cooler air at the foot of the mountains.

This is the oldest known photograph of the old Burke County Courthouse, made about 1890, and taken from the South Sterling Street side of the building. Note the spare four-sided roof cap.

The Burke County Courthouse was remodeled in 1903, about the time this photograph was made. The project included the addition of an elaborate cupola, which has become a current symbol for the county.

This view of Morganton, taken about 1867 from the grounds of the state mental hospital (Broughton Hill), shows the Burke County Courthouse at the upper center of the photograph.

Another very early view shows the courthouse between 1878 and 1903. Note the fence and steps around the Courthouse Square.

The view in this stylized postcard, entitled "Before the Fire - Dec. 13, 1893," looks westward along Union Street and shows the Hunt House Hotel on the southwestern corner of Union and Sterling Streets. A town fire that year burned the hotel (which earlier had been known as the Walton House hotel), seven buildings, and the Morganton Baptist Church.

The Hunt House, built in 1869 as the Walton House, served as the office for the stagecoach line to Asheville, making it an attractive antebellum stopping point for travelers venturing further west. This is the site of the main Morganton branch of Wachovia Bank in 2001.

Aunt Mandy's Kitchen, on the northeastern corner of Union and Sterling Streets, across from the old Burke County Courthouse, was the last clapboard building in the block. Note the cement traffic island in the middle of the intersection.

Local contractor William H. Sloan was hired to erect the new baroque-style cupola on the Burke County Courthouse during the remodeling of 1901–1903. This photograph, dated about 1904, shows the Green Street (northeast) front of the building.

Built as a fire-resistant hotel in 1924, the Caldwell Hotel was located at the corner of East Union and Green Streets, across the street from the Burke County Courthouse. It had 4 floors and 53 rooms. Located on the former homesite of John Caldwell and his son, North Carolina governor Tod R. Caldwell, it was built by a group of Morganton business leaders called the Burke Hotel Company.

Adjacent to the Caldwell Hotel stood the Sigmon Service Station, photographed here in 1931 when Green Street traffic was divided by a grassy median studded with Morganton's famous mimosa trees.

Southward down Green Street on the block where the "new" Burke County Courthouse was erected in the 1970s stood this stately frame residence at the corner of West Concord and Green Streets.

The once-prominent Caldwell Hotel was demolished in August 1965 and a municipal parking lot erected to handle parking for both retail businesses and the adjacent Mimosa Theater.

Two
Downtown Morganton

Typical transportation in Morganton in the 1890s was a horse and buggy, as pictured here in the 100 block of East Union Street. This photograph was taken between 1888 and 1916.

This 1865 photograph of downtown Morganton, looking westward down Union Street, shows a Union soldier leaning against a post on the left side of the street. Note the "perfumery" sign hanging from the side of the Hunt House Hotel.

This undated accident scene on the 100 block of West Union Street includes an upended wagon on the sidewalk and an empty barrel in the unpaved street.

This view of the "Cornwell Corner," as it was commonly called because Cornwell Drug Store occupied the northwest quadrant for many years, shows Union Street in 1905. Electricity lines stretched through downtown just after the turn of the century. First National Bank (the site of Wachovia Bank in 2001) by this time had taken the site where the Walton House/Hunt House Hotel previously was located.

The 1914 Fourth of July Parade in downtown Morganton featured, amid many hand-decorated floats, representatives of the fire department walking with fire hoses coiled on a large caisson.

Kirksey Hardware and Furniture Co., seen in this 1913 photograph, featured stoves and ranges for sale and a delivery horse-and-wagon festooned for a parade. The store moved to several different locations; at this time, it was on East Union Street, opposite the courthouse.

A shipment of new cars is proudly lined up along the 100 block of West Union Street, c. 1913.

Morganton hoisted her "Welcome" banner frequently during the early part of the 20th century. This photograph, which also appears on the cover of this book, shows a parade in downtown Morganton welcoming visiting car magnate Henry Ford in 1912. Traveling with him is believed to be another pioneer of the early automobile industry, Harvey Firestone.

This view of Green Street, looking north, indicates a wide, unpaved tree-lined boulevard. The edge of the Morgan Hotel is at the right in this photograph made before 1911.

The Morgan Hotel, located on Green Street at the intersection of East Union Street (the site of Bank of America in 2001), was another inn that sprang up in the late 19th century to handle the stagecoach passengers traveling a route that ran from Fayetteville to Asheville.

Battling a raging fire in the center of Morganton's business district in the early years of the 20th century is a horse-drawn fire wagon. The smoke is coming from Morganton Hardware Co., which was in business for more than 100 years before closing its downtown location in 2001.

This is the rear of the home, located on the Pearson Block, of David Tate Sr. and his wife, Ann Elizabeth McCall. The structure was also home to John Henry Pearson from his birth in 1852 until 1892. Located on the northeastern corner of Union and Sterling Streets, this was a popular gathering spot a century ago, as it is today. The location is the 2001 site of Benjamin's men's clothing store.

In 1893 Isaac and Nathan Lazarus, brothers and Jewish merchants from Baltimore, set up business in downtown Morganton on East Union Street. Lazarus Brothers included a department store and a grocery department and remained in business, albeit in different locations, until the end of 1999.

After the Civil War, there was no banking facility of any kind in Burke County for 25 years. Then, in October 1889, the Piedmont Bank was established, an offshoot of the Morganton Land and Development Company that also negotiated with the Waldenses and their colonization in Burke County. The bank, located in the Pearson Block of Union Street, sat opposite the Burke County Courthouse. The depression of the 1890s, however, led to the bank's collapse on December 2, 1897. This photograph was made of the once-elegant bank building in the 1920s.

Mr. L.A. Ward, employed to drag and level Morganton's dirt streets with a team of horses, is pictured here hard at work along what is believed to be Green Street.

Another view of Green Street, looking northward from near the intersection of East Concord Street, shows the formal medians that divided the thoroughfare for much of the early part of the 20th century.

This Morganton Police Station, located on South Sterling Street on the Courthouse Square, offered law enforcement officers a visible satellite office in the 1930s and 1940s.

By the 1930s, downtown Morganton had begun to change. The West Union Street Service Station, offering Shell gasoline for sale, was located at the College Street intersection. Note "The Cedars," the home of Col. Samuel Tate, at left.

A half a century after the David Tate House (later Aunt Mandy's Kitchen) was removed, Spake Pharmacy occupied the attractive corner of Union and Sterling Streets. This photograph was made in the late 1940s.

The H.D. Leonhardt home, atop Leonhardt Hill on Highway 70 East, sat on the outer reaches of Morganton in the 1920s. The dirt road was the major thoroughfare between Morganton and Valdese.

Before the age of supermarkets, Morgantonians bought most of their groceries at neighborhood stores, such as the H.D. Leonhardt Store (the site of Oxford Antiques in 2001) on Highway 70 East.

Gas at 19¢ a gallon was offered at the filling station on East Union Street in the shadow of the Premiere Hosiery building (future site of a new Morganton City Hall). This view, photographed in the 1920s, is looking westward toward Morganton's business district.

Retail and commercial businesses thrived in downtown Morganton through most of the mid-20th century. This 1940 view of the western, tree-lined side of the 100 block of North Sterling Street features Cole Printing Co. and Eloise Shoppe.

Throughout much of the middle part of the century, *The News Herald* (located before 1961 on South Sterling Street) hosted Election Night returns. Townspeople would gather in the cordoned-off street in front of the newspaper building (the site of Mimosa Insurance Co. in 2001) to await election results from the county's precincts, or boxes.

The Burkemont Hotel, located on the northeast corner of Green and Collett Streets, was a dominant fixture in downtown Morganton for many years. First Union Bank occupied the site in 2001.

The former Morganton City Hall was located on North King Street beside the Morganton Community House. The building was razed in the early 1960s when a new city hall (renovated in 1974) was constructed on East Meeting Street.

J. Gordon Queen, a longtime columnist for *The News Herald* of Morganton and its environs, promoted the city and its inevitable development. He was known for saying, "Morganton will grow whether we like it or not."

For many years, Edward A. Greene sold "fresh meats and groceries" at his West Union Street store, pictured here in the 1930s. The choice location was later home to Radar's Cafe and, in 2001, the Sub Club. Greene operated his grocery business here from about 1900 until 1933.

This was the first brick building constructed in Morganton. The photo, believed to have been taken in the early 1890s, shows the building on West Union Street that later became part of Morganton Hardware. Note the "customers" on horseback.

This view, looking west along Union Street, was taken early in the 20th century. Note the bank building at left where the Walton House/Hunt House Hotel once stood, and the Cornwell Corner at right.

A few years following the date of the photograph on the preceding page, Morganton erected ornamental lampposts with globe-clustered lights to illuminate West Union Street.

This 1920s view from atop the Caldwell Hotel looks westward down Union Street.

Three
SCHOOLS AND CHURCHES

Before 1903, general education in Burke County was sporadic at best, although private or subscription schools attracted well-trained, well-educated teachers. Among these was Robert Logan Patton who, after graduating from Amherst College, returned to his native Burke County in 1876 to teach at Table Rock Academy (pictured here) in Upper Creek Township. He was also a Baptist minister and head of a long line of exceptional educators in the county.

Rutherford Academy was established some time before 1850 in the village of Excelsior. (The hamlet later changed its name to the Town of Rutherford College, a name it bears to this day.) In its beginnings, the school was located in a one-room cabin called Owl Hollow School House. As the school grew and prospered, this larger facility was built, about 1859. The school closed during the Civil War, but re-opened between 1868 and 1869, about the time this photograph was made.

The Reverend Logan Patton, who began teaching at Table Rock Academy in the 1870s, taught at various schools throughout Burke and the surrounding counties. In 1891 he opened the West Morganton School, also known as the R.L. Patton School or Patton Academy, located on Anderson Street.

Bridgewater School, in western Burke County near the mouth of Muddy Creek, was one of many community-based schools of the early part of the 20th century. It closed in May 1922.

This is a photograph of a Glen Alpine school, possibly a subscription academy in operation in Glen Alpine before 1888.

The faculty at Rutherford College in the late 19th century included many competent teachers. Its first catalogue in 1880 boasted an advanced college curriculum.

This class at Joy School—located ten miles northwest of Morganton—like many in its era in the early part of the century taught little beyond reading, writing, and basic numbers.

North Carolina governor Charles B. Aycock, elected in 1901 on an education platform, helped turn the public's attitude toward a more educated citizenry. Still by the turn of the century, most of the schools in Burke County were one- or two-teacher institutions; this classroom at Piedmont Springs on Upper Creek in northwest Burke County was typical.

Grace Episcopal Church founded 11 mission houses throughout Burke County beginning about 1895. Most offered not only worship services, but school and some medical/social service outreach care as well. Mrs. George Hilton, wife of the rector of Grace Church, is pictured here in 1917 with a mountain family in the Pea Ridge area (where The Cross mission was established).

A successor to the Rutherford Academy, Rutherford College was chartered in 1871 with the right to confer degrees. It was located in southeastern Burke County in the village of Excelsior, which was chartered as a community in 1881, complete with a post office. Run by Rev. Robert Laban Abernathy, a Methodist, the college (like the school before it) drew its name from benefactor John Rutherford Jr., a bachelor at the time and one of the county's wealthiest men. The college offered free tuition for orphans, ministers' children, or prospective ministers. Ten years later, fire destroyed the building and a new facility was erected in 1893, about the time this photograph was made. In 1899 the building was sold to the Western North Carolina Methodist Conference, which operated the institution as a high school, and later a junior college. It ceased operations in the early 1930s.

Grace Episcopal Church was chartered in 1845 and this small clapboard, shuttered church was constructed in 1847 at the site of the current church on South King Street. It accommodated about 50 worshippers.

Gilboa Church, south of Morganton, was the first Methodist church site mentioned in early Burke County history, but in the city itself, Methodists shared use of the brick Presbyterian church, erected in 1820. In 1846 a small frame church was constructed near the site of the present Calvary Lutheran Church on North King Street. Fifty years later on April 5, 1896, during an Easter celebration, a large area of the church floor, having rotted, dropped to the ground, injuring several and shaking up most of the crowd. The incident led to the construction of a new brick church, pictured here, a couple of blocks south on King Street, opposite The Cedars. The first service was held there in October 1902. After World War II and a surge in membership, a larger church was built on the old Collett homeplace on the southeastern corner of King and Queen Streets. It was completed in 1952; a large addition was finished in 1992.

In the early 1890s, the congregation of Grace Episcopal Church decided its frame church was "too small and not sufficiently grand architecturally." The new church, built of native stone in the English Country Gothic style, was erected on the site of the old church; it was completed in 1894. This photograph was made in the early 1900s.

St. Margaret's Mission (sometimes called the Mill School) was established by Grace Episcopal Church in 1903 for the workers at the Alpine Cotton Mills. The mill furnished the school room, including desks. It was located below the railroad station on a hill behind the present-day Burger King at the intersection of Sterling Street and Fleming Drive. The building became an interdenominational chapel in 1935; a year later it was deconsecrated as a church. Its altar and many furnishings were given to the new stone St. Mary's Church, consecrated in 1940.

St. Stephen's Colored Episcopal Church was begun in 1891 and located across the street from the Grace Episcopal Churchyard on McDowell Street, then a narrow, muddy, rutted road. The word "colored" was later dropped from the name. The church was consecrated in 1894, and men from Grace Church's Brotherhood of St. Andrew provided early teachers and lay readers. A one-room school, between the church and the rectory, was the only school for African Americans in Morganton at the time. In 1949 the building was sold and a new church was erected on Bouchelle Street near the old Pearson ice house. This photo was made around the turn of the century.

The First Presbyterian Church educational building on Collett Street behind the old church was constructed in 1926. After the church moved to its new location on West Union Street, this building and property were sold to the First United Methodist Church in 1966 and subsequently torn down.

Members of the Presbyterian Church were active in Burke County in the late 18th century, but the first church building was not constructed in Morganton until the early 1820s. This exterior view of the church in the snow was probably made a few years before the church was remodeled and painted white in 1910. The building was located on the southwestern corner of North Sterling and Collett Streets and was razed in 1961.

Although the Baptists had been active in Burke County since about 1800, it was 1879 before the Morganton Baptist Church was organized with 12 members. The town fire of 1893 destroyed the first frame church on Sterling Street, just south of the Queen Street intersection, but a handsome new brick structure was built on the northeastern corner of South King and Meeting Streets in 1895 (pictured above). The First Baptist Church was expanded and beautified several times over the next 50 years. During the 1950s the church acquired the homeplaces of John H. Pearson, H.L. Milner, and A.M. Kistler on West Union Street, extending west to Riverside Drive. In 1967 the first service was held in the new $1.25 million church home.

This photograph, taken prior to the First Presbyterian Church's 1910 remodeling and expansion, shows the interior of the old church.

When the North Carolina Legislature decided to build a separate school for deaf children in 1891, a group of local men offered the state $5,000 and 100 acres of land adjoining Morganton's Vine Hill for the site. The state accepted and the money was raised through a special town bond election. The North Carolina School for the Deaf at Morganton opened on October 2, 1894 with 104 pupils; this photograph was taken about that time. Through the years the facilities have expanded to accommodate a growing enrollment, which reached its peak of more than 500 students in the mid-1960s. Enrollment, however, has declined in recent years.

The North Carolina School for the Deaf, pictured above, opened in 1894. It sat atop Vine Hill, the one-time home of Israel Pickens, and afforded pristine views of several area mountain ranges. It was at this stop in 1879 that the Episcopal Church attempted, unsuccessfully, to set up a college for African-American students. One building was constructed and it was to have been known as Ravenscroft or Wilberforce College, but insufficient funds sank the project.

This picture of the Morganton Graded School of 1935 was typical of its era, with children lined up in neat rows. The school was located at the corner of Avery Avenue and Bouchelle Street. The building was renovated in the 1980s and is used now for county offices.

Pictured here is the boys basketball team of 1933 at Bethel School.

The girls basketball team at Morganton High School is pictured in 1935.

The football team at Valdese High School posed for this picture in 1931. At that time the school was located at the Old Rock School.

Four
BURKE COUNTY AT WORK

Although farming has long been an integral part of the life of Burke County, the sad truth is that the geography and the terrain in the North Carolina foothills make such an enterprise difficult. Following the Civil War, independent farmers have had small successes, but by-and-large, the area is too hilly or too rocky for all but the most determined individual. A more realistic scenario finds more workers entering into growing industries, but farming a little on the side.

The Henderson Grist Mill, pictured here in 1912, was a landmark on Upper Creek in northern Burke County for more than half a century. Most of the grain was ground for a specific customer, with the miller getting paid in a percentage of the ground grain.

The thick forests of Burke County, which had been a hindrance to pioneer farming, became a source of industry after the Civil War and the growth of many small sawmill operations throughout the county, such as this one at Wolf Pitt.

Around 1910, unimproved mountain land was selling for $5 to $10 an acre, depending on the volume of timber on it. Sawmills such as this operation flourished.

Gold was discovered in the southwestern part of Burke County in 1828, and for the next several years there was a frenzy of mining activity. There was never enough gold found to make such enterprises profitable for very long; however, from time to time, up until about 1920, new operations—some with mechanized equipment—surfaced. The barge pictured here was said to have been built to dredge for gold on the Catawba River, only there wasn't enough water to float it.

In 1895, Kistler, Lesh, and Company, which ran a tanning company in Pennsylvania, moved to Morganton to open the Burke Tannery. The operation continued until 1921, but only young Andrew M. Kistler, who had moved here in 1902, remained. He and his family continued to play an important part in the development of Morganton and Burke County through much of the 20th century.

Rows of bark and "acid wood" are stacked up at the Burke Tannery prior to 1920. The abundance of oak and chestnut wood in the county at the time was important to the industry.

Drexel Furniture Company was founded in 1903 near a sawmill site beside the Southern Railway, about six and a half miles east of Morganton. This photo was made about 1906 and shows the "new" plant. The original factory burned in 1905. The company remains one of Burke County's largest employers, and at one time was the world's largest manufacturer of quality dining room and bedroom furniture.

Skilled cabinet makers and woodworkers were already fixtures in Morganton when the Morganton Furniture Manufacturing Co. was established in 1885. The plant, located on the Western North Carolina Railroad line, was destroyed by fire in 1887.

In the mid-1890s, Alpine Cotton Mill grew out of the failure of its predecessor, Dunavant Cotton Mill, and was located across from the Morganton depot. Some 50 years later the mill was acquired by Drexel Furniture Company, which converted the textile operation into furniture manufacturing.

A crew from W.H. Queen's painter and paperhanger business poses outside a newly completed residence in the 1920s.

A c. 1906 picture of a construction crew shows the digging of the Marion Tunnel for the Carolina, Clinchfield and Ohio Railroad.

Shortly after the close of the Civil War, the Western North Carolina Railroad reached the town of Morganton. Here, a wood-burning locomotive and cars are leaving the town's first railroad depot, constructed about 1875.

Morganton's second town depot, constructed about 1890, is pictured here with horse-drawn carriages awaiting the arrival of passengers on the Western North Carolina Railroad.

Sometime around 1920 a group of new automobiles for sale is delivered and lined up for public inspection on the unpaved and rutted West Union Street, near Gaither's Garage.

"Aunt Nancy Jones" was an herb doctor and midwife in the 19th century who preceded the presence of professional nurses in the area. She was on call to the whole community, both black and white. Her custom was to remain in the home several days after a child was born until everyone was accustomed to the new baby.

When a statewide prohibition on the manufacture of distilled spirits went into effect in 1909, a number of illegal distilling or "moonshining" operations began in the mountains and backwoods of Burke County. These corn liquor operations were relatively plentiful until about the middle of the 20th century.

These two unidentified employees of Kirksey and Co. Funeral Home stand over a casket canopy, perhaps a forerunner to the family tent frequently used today at graveside funeral services.

Fire was indeed a curse in Burke County, with the number of furniture manufacturing operations located here. This one, in the 1930s, appears to be under control at the time of this photograph.

In June 1936, this fire at the Morganton Furniture Company Veneer Plant shot flames and smoke high into the air. Again, by the time the photograph was made, the fire appears to have been contained.

A Kirksey and Company employee proudly poses with a new ambulance that was delivered on June 1, 1930.

Employees of Burke Furniture Company enjoy a banquet at the old Burkemont Hotel Dining Room in 1937.

Morganton Hardware Company's 50th anniversary celebration in 1946 drew a crowd to its downtown store, not only for the sale, but for cake and refreshments as well.

After World War II, the demand for quality-made clothing soared. At this Betty Lou Shop sale, early morning customers have to nudge their way through the merchandise. Store owners Mose and Ruth Adler are pictured at the far right.

During the Great Depression, a Civilian Conservation Corps (CCC) Camp was set up at Enola and housed some 200 young men, aged 18 to 25. They lived in tents and were under military personnel supervision; at work, they were under the aegis of the U.S. Forest Service. The CCC employed these men to clean up watersheds, build Forest Service roads, help control soil erosion, and fight fires, if necessary.

In 1933, the CCC youth lived in tents in their Enola campsite and found an income in the job-scarce economy of the time. Their work services also included building lookout posts and stringing telephone lines to the posts.

Camp Dyer in the Enola section of Burke County was home to more than 200 young men during the Great Depression.

Duke Power Company built Lake James during the period of 1916 to 1923 by creating three dams and using the water from the Catawba and Linville Rivers as well as Paddy's Creek. The lake, named for company pioneer James B. Duke, has 152 miles of shoreline. Its power station, shown here in the 1940s, is located at the Linville River dam.

Building Lake James took seven years. Its surface area is more than 6,500 acres. For its construction, the entire town of Fonta Flora (population of about 50 people), located 13 miles northwest of Morganton, was covered by the lake's waters.

To facilitate the construction of the new Lake James, teams of horses were used to cut roads and a complete railroad was built to haul dirt that was excavated from the canal to build the dam.

Construction of Lake James was difficult work that lasted seven years. Another community, Gibbs (population about 25) on Paddy's Creek, was also submerged in the new giant lake.

This view of the construction of the Linville River dam at Lake James, taken about 1920, illustrates of the massiveness of the lake.

An early photograph shows the powerhouse at Lake James, c. 1923.

This 1949 view of Ebony Funeral Home on Avery Avenue shows the property studded with trees. Later expansions and renovations have altered the facade.

An ice scraper cleans West Union Street in this vintage 1950s photograph that also shows Lazarus Department Store in the background. Lazarus later moved to a free-standing building at the corner of North Sterling Street and Avery Avenue. The store closed at the end of the 20th century.

Some years earlier, in the 1930s, municipal workers clean up West Union Street, albeit at a different location—the 100 block of West Union. At the time, Morganton referred to herself as the "Town" (not "City") of Morganton.

Five
BURKE COUNTY AT PLAY

Participating in one of Morganton's annual parades, this 1939 float features a flowered key to the city atop the Chamber of Commerce and Merchants Association float.

Morgantonians love to celebrate with parades through the city. This parade float from the Alpine Cotton Mills features employees costumed and seated in front of banked fibers the plant manufactured.

Baseball has long been one of Burke County's favorite recreational pastimes. Here, in 1910, the Linville baseball team poses for a photograph after having defeated Morganton's first team, 8-5.

Here is one of Morganton's baseball teams in 1910, pictured on the old Avery Avenue playing field. We don't know whether or not this is the team that Linville (see page 86) defeated.

In 1919, for its Independence Day Celebration, aviator Henry Westall of Asheville made a daring flight to Morganton in less than an hour.

Aviator and stunt flyer Henry Westall of Asheville took up passengers for flights aboard this double-wing aircraft, in town for the Fourth of July celebration.

The 1919 Independence Day parade feature horses and wagons, such as this one pictured, and later, public events that included climbing a greased pole and catching a greased pig.

Children in a pony-driven car, all decorated with flags and festoons, were part of the famous 1919 Independence Day parade.

Held immediately after World War I, Morganton's 1919 Independence Day parade was a major public gathering. Uniformed soldiers marched through downtown Morganton to the beat of a brass band and cheering crowds.

For the 1919 Independence Day parade, Kirksey and Company provided its own music and featured a gramophone atop its float, which promoted the Columbia recording of "Our Boys in Camp."

A large consignment of young people were costumed as Native Americans for the "Mother Burke" pageant, performed in the 1920s.

We don't know the script of the "Mother Burke" pageant, but this photograph shows colonial soldiers being held at bay by a gun-toting "Mother Burke."

The new Bridgewater bridge, still incomplete, became a notable backdrop for photographs in the early 1920s. The bridge was built as part of the construction of Lake James.

This unidentified family poses for a photograph on Burke County's new bridge over the Catawba River at Bridgewater

These bathing beauties take advantage of the cool water at the Valdese Pool in the 1930s.

The Valdese Pool operated for many years as a recreational mecca used by many in Burke County to escape the warmth of summer prior to the age of air conditioning.

Morganton fielded her own semi-pro baseball team in the late 1940s and early 1950s—the Morganton Aggies. The team is pictured here in 1951.

Constructed by the Civil Works Administration, a New Deal program, in 1934, the Morganton Community House has long been a centerpiece for social and civic gatherings. This is a 1950 view of the building before a major expansion and renovation in the early 1980s.

Burke County has a distinct reputation for political activism. Perhaps the large number of state employees plays a part, or perhaps it is a manifestation of the county's independent spirit. This scene is from a 1936 Democratic Rally, and the sign on the donkey reads, "We Want Roosevelt Again."

Another view from the same 1936 Democratic Rally, on October 23, is an indication of Burke County's participation in political affairs.

In the early part of the century, it was commonplace for circuit-riding photographers to travel from house to house with a pony and entice families to have their picture made with the visiting animal.

Family photography was rare in the early part of the 20th century and called for the family to don their best clothes. Note the knickers on the young man and boy at left and the knee stockings on the girls.

Six

THE WALDENSES SETTLEMENT

Waldensian members of *Le Phare Des Alpes* ("the lighthouse of the Alps") are pictured here July 4, 1917, at their annual Independence Day dinner. The organization is a mutual aide society of Valdese, founded in 1909, and limited to men of Waldensian descent. The Waldenses, Protestant Italians living in the high valleys of the Cottian Alps in northern Italy, near the French border, emigrated to Valdese in 1893 largely because of overcrowding in their homeland. Having purchased 10,000 acres of land eight miles east of Morganton from the Morganton Land and Development Company, the first of three contingents of Waldenses arrived May 29, 1893. The early settlement was operated as a commune.

This view of the Valdese train station in 1915 shows a train arriving from the west. The nearby house was hastily constructed in 1893 to accommodate the third contingent of Waldensians who were expected in November of that year. Located at the corner of Massel Avenue and Faet Street, the house became multi-functional for the colonists, serving as a sanctuary for worship services, a school for the bilingual children, a post office, and a retail store, meeting the business needs of the colony.

On March 27, 1897, the wedding party at the marriage of Jean-Henri Pascal and Louise Pons posed for this photograph. Pictured, from left to right, are (front row) Marie Pons Refour, Jaubert Micol, Susanne Pons Pascal, Samuel Pons, Susanne Pascal Pons, Jean-Henri Pascal (groom), Louise Pons Pascal (bride), and Jeannette Pons; (back row) Henriette Perrou Bouchard, Rev. Barthelemy Soulier, Marianne Micol Tron, Francoise Pascal, Emmanuel Tron, and Madeleine Giraud Micol.

The first contingent of Waldensian settlers (29 of them) missed the *pain quotodien* (daily bread) that they were accustomed to baking in outdoor ovens. This one was built soon after the first colonists arrived in 1893 and served the colonists for months until each family could build their own oven to share with neighbors. Holding the ladle is Jean Jacques Leger. The oven was located on what is now Rodoret Street on a site east of the present-day post office.

The Waldenses came from the Waldensian Church in Italy, the oldest evangelical church in existence (predating the Reformation by at least 400 years). In the United States, the Waldensians affiliated with the Presbyterian Church and began construction on their church building, a Romanesque design similar to their home churches, in 1897. The sanctuary was completed two years later and dedicated July 4, 1899, about the time this photograph was made.

Before building their church, the early Waldensian settlers nonetheless worshipped faithfully together. Here, a Sunday school group in 1894 meets on Arnaud Avenue between Italy and Rodoret Streets.

Waldensian women, dressed in their native attire, posed for this photograph at the Burke County Pageant, held in Morganton on May 15, 1924. Sunday attire consisted of a white coiffe, a basic dark dress with apron, and a shoulder shawl and pin at the neckline bearing the Waldensian emblem. Pictured here, from left to right, are (front row) Irma Ghigo Rostan, John Tron, Rachel Perrou, and Margaret Gardiol; (back row) Susanne Martinat, Susanne Giraud, Lydia Jacumin Pons, Lydia Parise, Adele Bouchard Tron, Marianne Garrou Pons, Amandine Bouchard Saunders, Mary Grill, Helen Grill, and Mary Martinat.

The Valdese train station is pictured in the 1920s. It remained the center of the colony (later the town) of Valdese for many years. By the time this photograph was made, the settlement included more than 40 nearby farms. In addition to wheat, corn, and vegetables, most of these farm families cultivated about an acre in grapes, each producing 400 to 600 gallons of wine.

The Waldensian Hosiery Mills, pictured here in 1902, was the first textile mill in Valdese. The original plant was constructed of timber cut from the owner's farmlands and covered with corrugated metal. Company founders were John "Bobo" Garrou Sr., Francis Garrou Sr., and Antoine Grill. The mill was located near the Southern Railway tracks. Twenty employees worked at a wage of 40¢ to 50¢ a day for the men and boys, and 35¢ for the women. In 1961 the company merged with Alba Hosiery Mills into Alba-Waldensian, Inc., and became a public company.

The first bakery in Valdese opened in 1915 with two employees, John P. Rostan and Fillippe Ghigo, brothers-in-law who had worked in bakeries in New York City but had decided to join their countrymen in the Waldensian colony in Valdese. Today the bakery employs more than 700 people and can produce enough bread daily to make sandwiches for the entire state of North Carolina.

The first bakery truck for Waldensian Bakery in Valdese advertised not only French and American bread, but also macaroni and spaghetti as well. Initially, it is said John P. Roston, one of the bakery founders, would bake bread at night, carry it in a wheelbarrow to the Valdese train station, ride the train to Morganton, and deliver it to customers on foot. At the end of the day he would walk the eight miles back home.

The Rock School, completed in 1923, was built of native stone by local Waldensian masons. It initially served as Valdese High School, as shown in this 1925 photograph. The school, now known as the Old Rock School, was extensively renovated in the 1980s and offers a variety of facilities that host everything from civic club meetings to community plays and concerts.

The original Waldenses and succeeding generations have taken the game of *boccie* very seriously, as evidenced in this 1930s photograph. *Boccie* is a game similar to lawn bowling and played with wooden balls. Pictured here, from left to right, are Ben Perrou, Lee Ribet, John Salvaggio, Dick Pons, Daniel Rostan, Ben Pons, Henry J. Garrou, Dick Ribet, and Henry Curville.

McGalliard Falls, located on McGalliard Creek north of Valdese, remains a popular recreation site in Burke County. Fred Meytre operated a water mill here in 1908.

Seven

LANDMARKS

THEN AND NOW

The Council Oak was a longstanding landmark in Burke County until the 20th century. Under this giant oak tree in Quaker Meadows, Overmountain Men (volunteers), under the leadership of Charles and Joseph McDowell, met in council before going out to meet General Ferguson at the Battle of Kings Mountain. That battle was a disaster for the Tories and a turning point for the American patriots in the Revolutionary War.

The Cedars, long known as the Tate House, was built in 1840 on the corner of King and West Union Streets in downtown Morganton. This photo was made before the 1875 remodeling, which included the addition of a front tower and a mansard-style roof.

The White Parlor at the Tate House was one of several elaborately furnished rooms in the house. Listed on the National Register of Historic Places, the house remained a family dwelling until the 1990s. In 2001, it was being renovated as a commercial savings and loan association.

Creekside, the antebellum home of Col. Thomas G. Walton, remains today a private residence occupied by Walton family descendants. Colonel Walton's brother, William M. Walton, built an identical residence, Brookwood, several miles further west, near Carbon City, but the latter was burned in a fire in 1920.

Grace Hospital was founded in 1906 and was located on the old Mumford property on three acres of land, opposite the Grace Episcopal Church rectory on King and McDowell Streets. The founders of the hospital were Rev. Walter Hughson (Grace Church rector), his wife, Mary, and Rev. Edward W. Phifer Sr., resident physician. There were eight beds and one crib in each ward and a private room in the main building; an annex contained two wards of four beds each for African-American patients. The hospital also had an operating room and a dispensary. During its first year, 72 people received care. This photograph of the original hospital would have been taken about 1910; it was in that year that missionary nurse Maria Allen established the Grace Hospital School of Nursing.

This new 62-bed, 4-story brick hospital was built on the old Grace Hospital site, facing College Street, in 1929. It was expanded and remodeled several times, but in 1973 the hospital was relocated some three miles south of downtown Morganton, near Interstate 40.

Front View, Western Hospital for the Insane, Morganton, N. C.

A growing demand for care and accommodations for the state's mentally ill led to the construction of a second asylum for the insane—the first was built in Raleigh in 1858. In 1883 the Western Insane Asylum of North Carolina was established in Morganton, thought it was later known as Broughton Hospital. For many years the hospital ran its own dairy, farm, and laundry, even supplying produce and dairy products to other state facilities.

In 1901 psychiatrist Dr. Isaac Montrose Taylor and two other physicians acquired the James A. Claywell property on Valdese Avenue in Morganton and established Broadoaks Sanitorium, a private institution for the care of the mentally ill. On April 3, 1924, a major fire claimed the lives of four patients. The facility, pictured in 1931, continued to provide in-patient care until 1959.

This turn-of-the-century postcard shows some of the elaborate residential homes built along Morganton's West Union Street, west of the city. Many are still standing today.

This building, later called Cedar Grove Cottage, was built in 1875 by Col. Samuel McDowell Tate as a school for children. Located on the corner of South King and Meeting Streets, it was remodeled in 1934 by Charles Gordon Tate and used as a family residence until it was torn down in 1992.

Pleasant Valley plantation, located on 400 acres of land lying on Johns River and the Piedmont Road, was built in 1829 by Alfred Perkins, the grandson of "Gentleman" John Perkins, one of Burke County's pioneer landholders. The two-story brick home overlooks fertile bottom lands along the river.

This timeless view of the Linville Gorge was actually photographed about 75 years ago, but could just as easily have been pictured today. The gorge, located in the northwest part of the county, begins at Linville Falls. The "walls" of the gorge—long a favorite, though dangerous, destination for hikers and campers—are formed by Linville Mountain on the west and by Jonas Ridge on the east, both spur extensions of the Blue Ridge Mountain Range, emanating from Grandfather Mountain.

Piedmont Springs Hotel, located on Upper Creek about three miles north of the Steels Creek–Upper Creek area, was the only overnight inn in Burke County before the Civil War. Natural sulfur springs drew visitors to the hotel's 28 rooms. The Great Flood of 1916 destroyed the hotel, which had ceased accepting guests in the 1890s.

The Glen Alpine Springs Hotel, located on Hall Creek in the southwestern mountains of Burke County, was established in 1878. It was said to be the largest frame building in the state, housing some 100 guests. It is not known when the hotel ceased operations, but the building was burned in 1936. Look closely in the foreground to see a lady holding a horse by the reins.

A mineral spring in the middle of the village of Connelly Springs led to the construction of the Connelly Springs Hotel in 1886. The hotel flourished in the 1890s as the water from the spring (set apart with a latticework spring house) enjoyed an international reputation as a tonic for kidney and bladder disease. The two-story building was studded with cottages built along a path to the spring, and a ballroom and bowling alley were added. The dining room accommodated 100 guests and string music was provided during dinner. The hotel declined after the turn of the century, and it was demolished during World War II.

The Crites family of six took time to sit for a photograph in 1902 while they were staying at one of Burke County's Victorian-era mineral springs hotels, thought to be Piedmont Springs Hotel. Sterling Crites, age two, is seated on his father's lap.

Sitting Bear rock formation, one of a series of odd rock forms along the edge of Jonas Ridge, is the northernmost along this spar of the Appalachian Mountains.

The hamlet of Mortimer at the Burke County–Caldwell line was an attractive mountain retreat in the early part of the 20th century.

Eight
Burke County Distinctions

In 1916 torrential rains flooded Burke County's creeks, rivers, and roads, including the Catawba River. This famous photograph of W. Dwight Rust delivering the mail on a makeshift pulley across the swollen waterway highlights the vulnerability of the communities in the river valley.

Dozens of townspeople flocked to the banks of the Catawba to witness the raging water during the Flood of 1916. In his book, *Tales of Old Burke*, J. Alex Mull (who was seven years old at the

time) later wrote "I saw what looked like a barn floating down the river like a steamboat with a lone rooster on top, and large trees tossed about like matchsticks."

The Allman Smith Blacksmith Shop is pictured here during the Flood of 1916, all but submerged by the vast spread of water from the Catawba and other streams.

The Flood of 1916 not only washed away homes, bridges, and roads, but it tore up railroad tracks as well. Communications and transportation both north and west were shut down for weeks. One example of the ferocity of the flood, Fons Duckworth's store, a two-story brick building with a flat roof, was all but covered when the water rose to the top of the building. Duckworth was rescued, but others were not so fortunate.

On August 13, 1900, two Southern Railroad trains collided head-on two miles west of Morganton at the Hennessee dip. These photos show the extensive damage to both trains.

It is unclear who or what was at fault in the 1900 Southern Railroad collision of two trains—the westbound Engine No. 53, with Bob Means as engineer, and the eastbound Engine No. 37, with engineer Alexander M. Gabriel.

Chapter four in this book gives some examples of the work that went into the building of Lake James between 1916 and 1923. At the time, this was the largest dirt dam ever built in the world, and finding laborers was an ongoing problem. Convicts were brought in along with workers from South Carolina, Georgia, and Alabama. When women were brought in to handle the cooking and housekeeping, fights—even killings—broke out among the men. It is said bodies were dumped into the dam and covered with dirt.

Burke County's most famous son is the late U.S. Senator Sam J. Ervin Jr., noted lawyer, jurist, statesman, and author, who in this 1954 photograph is shown arriving at the train station in Washington, D.C. with his family. Pictured, from left to right, are daughters Laura and Lesley, the senator, Mrs. Ervin, daughter-in-law Betty, and son, the late Sam J. Ervin III (later a U.S. Court of Appeals judge, known locally as "Sam Three-I").

U.S. Senator Sam J. Ervin Jr. chaired the 1973 Senate Select Committee on Presidential Campaign Activities, more commonly referred to as the "Watergate Committee." He is pictured here during one of the nationally televised hearings on abuses of powers that led to the resignation of President Richard Nixon.

Senator Ervin's Bible-quoting, "I'm-just-a-country-lawyer" demeanor failed to hide the Morganton native's genius. After graduating from the University of North Carolina and serving with distinction in World War I, he was the only student ever to go through Harvard Law School backwards—that is, he took his third-year coursework first and his first-year curriculum last.

Acknowledgments

When I moved to Morganton in 1979 to become editor of *The News Herald*, my predecessor, the late W. Stanley Moore, took me under his wing. My first week here, Stanley and the late Dr. Edward W. Phifer Jr., Burke County's consummate historian, invited me to a shindig at Ivey Griffin's place near Shortoff Mountain. I spent the evening sipping white liquor and basking in the company of some of Burke County's legendary storytellers, including the late "Doggie" Hatcher. It was an extraordinary experience; I laughed so hard my face hurt. And that night I became a disciple of the lore and legends of this magnificent spot on God's good earth.

We are indebted to a number of individuals and institutions for their generous and prodigious support of this project. Specifically, I would like to thank the following people who have kindly loaned photographs: Historic Burke Foundation, and particularly Fluff Manderson, executive director, for the loan of the Joe Lineberger collection of photographs and postcards; Burke County Library, the Burke County Historical Society, and especially Gail Benfield, curator of the North Carolina Room; Susan Fitz Rhodes, daughter of the late J.D. Fitz, for the loan of the Walt Green collection of Morganton photographs and negatives (J.D., who had inherited the Green collection, was the longtime publisher of *The News Herald* and my first boss here. Like his great friend, Stanley Moore, he helped cement my affection for this community.); Mrs. Jewel Bounous and the Waldensian Museum, whose remarkable historical archives ought to be viewed and studied as a mandatory part of the curriculum of every student in Burke County; L.H. Kirksey, for the loan of a number of photographs and memorabilia from Kirksey Funeral Home and Kirksey Hardware Company, two of Burke County's pioneer businesses; Leroy Leonhardt, whose grandfather, Dewey M. Leonhardt, had worked as a commercial photographer in the 1920s and 1930s and had amassed a wonderful assortment of pictures; the Episcopal Diocese of Western North Carolina, Grace Episcopal Church, the First Baptist Church and Barbara Lambert, First United Methodist Church and Margaret Causby, and First Presbyterian Church for photographs, monographs, and texts of their respective institutions; the late J. Alex Mull, whose out-of-print book, *Tales of Old Burke*, was an invaluable resource; and the late Dr. Edward W. Phifer Jr., whose book, *Burke: The History of a North Carolina County*, is the ultimate authority on this county's illustrious past.

I would also like to acknowledge the numerous men and women who kindly stepped in to assist in identifying or confirming dates, location, and details of many of the photos selected in this volume.

And finally, thanks to my wife, Sherry Bush Willard, herself a native of these majestic foothills (albeit in Caldwell County), for her patience, support, and encouragement throughout this project.

—H. Eugene Willard

Visit us at
arcadiapublishing.com

www.ingramcontent.com/pod-product-compliance
Lightning Source LLC
Chambersburg PA
CBHW080903100426
42812CB00007B/2135